I0463261

Real Estate Blind Pools

Exempt offerings of $500,000 to $5,000,000 real estate projects

By: Douglas Slain, MA., JD.

Law Offices of Douglas Slain
59 Morning Sun Avenue, # A
Mill Valley CA 94941
T: 415-888-8289
F: 415-383-1766
privateplacementadvisors.com

Real Estate Blind Pools   : $14.95

Introduction

This handbook is for anyone seeking $500,000 to $5,000,000 to fund a real estate limited partnership without having to identify which properties will be bought, developed or sold on behalf of the investors. This form of investment is colloquially known as a blind pool.

Just as with a real estate investment trust (REIT) where investors do not know which properties the partnership will purchase, a blind pool limited partnership interest's valuation is based on the partnership's prospects-- which in turn are based on general partner's track record.

This is different than a specified asset partnership where an investment can be evaluated based on costs and projected revenues.

Interestingly, there is no evidence that the average performance of blind pools differs significantly from the performance of comparable specified asset partnerships.

For most real estate entrepreneurs the advantages of being able to raise money without having to first identify and have under contract a particular property are obvious. However, when hearing the word "securities" in connection with raising money for their particular deal, most react as 14th C. Flemish townsmen might have upon hearing of a new plague.

But securities can be a good thing. Showing sophistication about the securities component of your project can garner respect as well as expand the number of prospective investors, to say nothing of providing asset protection advantages down the road if things go south.

Rather than speculate on what specific real estate projects may be best for blind pool private placements (think location, location, and timing), this handbook discusses subjects relevant to anyone looking to fund a real estate project when financial institutions are out of the question.

Chapter one explains why this whole subject may actually be of interest to you; to wit, unless your money partner(s) are also operational decision-makers, you will be subject to California and possibly federal securities if you raise money.

Chapters two through six discuss the usual suspects or topics that need to be addressed in any effort to locate private sources of capital: structure of the deal, the offering documentation, and the how and why of the investor package.

Chapter seven is mostly of academic interest, but you should know about charging orders, a sort of legal outlier all on its own.

Chapters eight and nine cover remedies available to wronged investors in a real estate private placement.

Chapter ten addresses California real estate exempt offerings and private placements.

Chapter eleven discusses finders.

This is the first of a series of handbooks covering popular uses of exempt offerings and private placements.

Preface and Historical Note

Most people do not know that individual states were regulating securities fraud before the federal government got involved. Years before the S.E.C. was a glint in the eyes of U.S. legislators, state regulators were shutting down securities violators.

The term "blue sky" suggests the type of fraudulent activity targeted by the states almost 100 years ago when Justice McKenna used the phrase in 1917 to characterize "speculative schemes which have no more basis than so many feet of 'blue sky."

In *Hall vs. Geiger-Jones Co.*, 242 U.S. 539 (1917), the good judge wrote:

"The name that is given to the law indicates the evil at which it is aimed, that is, to use the language of a cited case, "speculative schemes which have no more basis than so many feet of 'blue sky'; or, as stated by counsel in another case, "to stop the sale of stock in fly-by-night concerns, visionary oil wells, distant gold mines and other like fraudulent exploitations'."

Even if the descriptions be regarded as rhetorical, the existence of evil is indicated, and a belief of its detriment; and we shall not pause to do more than state that the prevention of deception is within the competency of government and that the appreciation of the consequences of it is not open for our review."

While the SEC now is the chief enforcer of the nation's securities laws, each state has its own securities regime, known as its "Blue Sky Law," with its own enforcement apparatus in place.

Most states securities laws are modeled after the Uniform Securities Act of 1956; while some states may have identical statutory language or regulations, however, interpretations of the same words can differ from state to state. Before a security is sold there must be a registration in place to cover the transaction. Every offer or sale of a security must be registered or exempt from registration under blue sky laws of the state in which the security is offered.

Although many types of securities, and many transactions, are exempt from state securities registration under Regulation D (17 CFR § 230.501 et seq.), all states continue to require coordination or notice filings.

In any event, exemption never affects the ability of state regulators to investigate and to bring fraud charges. For some colorful examples of blue sky fraud, download the launch issue of *Securities Enforcement Reporter* at www.enforcementreporter.com.

Table of Contents

Chapter One: Real Estate Exempt Offerings

What is a private placement or exempt offering?

And why does it matter?

Shares of companies listed on public exchanges must have been approved by the S.E.C. and been qualified with state securities regulators. Those are public offerings.

If an individual or an existing company wants to be exempt from state qualification and Federal registration when raising money, it is a private offering. Such private placements include partnership interests and other familiar joint-ownership entities.

One example of a private offering is the Goldman-Sachs ill-advised exempt offering of Facebook.com shares.

Another example was my neighbor asking a few fraternity brothers to invest $150,000 each in a commercial rental putative "flip."

Another example is a movie production and distribution start-up where one friend asks another for $50,000 to help launch it.

Small or big, sexy deals or prosaic, $250,000 real estate limited partnership or $250,000,000 next-big-thing pre—

IPO Reg D offering (e.g., LinkedIn and Facebook in the summer of 2011), they are all private offerings.

The easiest way to think of it is this: If you are asking someone for money for some venture in which you are to do the work and the other person and/or other persons are to receive some benefit from their investment, you have created a security.

Why does that matter?

Because securities have to be registered or be exempt from registration.

What if they are not? I know lots of deals where fear of "securities violations" had nothing to do with it. Some of these deals were very profitable for the investors and no one said a word about private offerings or "exempt" anything.

You are right; usually it does not matter!

The vast majority of private deals are neither registered nor exempt from registration. In fact, so many private deals are not properly documented a state regulator once said, "There is a nation-wide crime wave going on and other than us guys no one knows about it."

Why bother to pay to do this right?

Because if the deal goes south, if anything at all goes wrong, you must return investors' money if they ask for it. And if the money is not there, a judgment will be

Page 10

entered against you no whatever how many LLCs or
other entities were created to avoid just such exposure.

In other words, if you do not bother to get the securities
compliance component right, any investor can ask for
their money back, at a minimum.

It also includes two chapters for wronged investors who
want to make use of California's potent Securities Act---
and serving as a cautionary tale for anyone availing
themselves of non-institutional money for real estate
projects.

Chapter Two: Business Plans

Business plans should be written as a form of deal evaluation.

Writing a good business plan is more than an exercise done to raise funds; it is an actual planning exercise, a thoughtful review of the viability of your venture.

View your business plan as a process to express your ideas as opposed to a chore you dread doing. Make your plan reflect your passion and commitment.

Communicate the viability of your idea but be modest in your promises.

Business plans written in this manner allow the integrity and sincerity of the writer to show through.

Investors will always reject exaggerated claims. After that, they will begin to doubt underlying business acumen and integrity.

A good business plan does not need to be long. Twenty to thirty pages often gets the job done. Do not start by writing the executive summary. Start with an outline of your ideas. Then write the plan. Then the executive summary should write itself.

Your executive summary should summarize the plan, not anticipate it.

Here is a template for organizing your thoughts.

I. COMPANY PURPOSE

II. THE PROBLEM

III. THE SOLUTION

IV. WHY NOW

V. MARKET SIZE

VI. COMPETITION

VII. PRODUCTS/SERVICES

VIII. BUSINESS MODEL

IX. MANAGEMENT

X. EXIT STRATEGY

XI. FINANCING

XII. EXECUTIVE SUMMARY

Chapter Three: Structure

How much of the equity and/or profits for the investors and how much for you and/or your company?

Which state or states in which to incorporate your LLCs?

Answer these questions and you have decided on the structure of your fund.

You understandably want to keep as much of the opportunity as you can for yourself. But if you miscalculate how much outsiders' money it will take, you run the risk of having to raise additional sums of money in the future rather than manage the business, or risk failing altogether.

You also need to decide which corporate entity to use.

The tax advantages and flexibility provided by LLCs are well known; most California real estate operators use Nevada or California entities.

Practice tip: It turns off investors when you get too clever in taking advantage of the flexibility of multiple LLCs.

Keep it simple.

Chapter Five: Preparing to Raise

Now you need an investor presentation. An investor presentation simply consists of your printed hand-outs (and power point presentation if you have one) for meetings with potential investors.

A presentation can be structured as follows:

1) Describe your real estate project or fund and describe how it is better than competitive choices, if any.

2) Describe how the cost of your property or properties is less than the value of the benefit created, relative either to competitors' solutions or, if your property addresses an unmet need, to the current state of affairs for buyers.

5) Having described the value proposition for a single customer, describe your initial target market.

6) Describe your sales strategy.

7) Present a 3-year projection of revenues, gross margins, earnings, and cash flow. Estimate the month you will achieve positive cash flow and positive earnings.

9) Explain the existing capital structure, who owns

what, who will own what, and any unique terms.

Explain why you need money now and how much money, if any, you may need in the future.

10) Communicate your valuation by expressing it as a multiple of revenues or earnings, using comparable transactions, or by some other method.

11) Recap why you have a credible story and why the investment risk versus opportunity equation is fair and reasonable.

Prepare a due diligence binder in which you collect in one place all of the pieces of paper that a seasoned investor might want to see to complete his due diligence, including copies of articles of incorporation, leases, employment agreements, option agreements,

Keep in mind that it can take some time to complete this chore as the relevant documents may be located in numerous places. As with the presentation, you can work on the due diligence binder while completing other steps in the process.

Eventually, you will need to file with the S.E.C. under Regulation D (assuming you are using this exemption) and also file in each state in which you plan to contact investors. Most Reg D applicants wait up to the maximum time permitted (15 days) after an investor has signed up before filing.

Chapter Six: Raising Money

You are finally ready to raise some money.

Who do you have in mind?

LinkedIn discussion group contacts?

Friends and family members?

Self-directed IRA seminars where you are one of several presenters?

Every time you identify a potential investor, send an appropriate email with your executive summary. Do not appear to be in a hurry. Record all contacts on spreadsheet. Follow up by telephone a few days later. You will get turned down most of the time, but some investors will ask for more information. At meetings, you will "present" as described in Preparing.

Typically, entrepreneurs spend weeks or even months researching, emailing, and phoning before they do much presenting but if you have your documentation organized go ahead and present as soon as you can.

There's no silver bullet, regardless of the quality of your deal. You can hire a finder in some form (see the last chapter of this handbook) who may be able to get you in front of people, but you will still need to present your business idea and yourself.

Chapter Seven: Charging Orders

Limited liability companies are the entity of choice for most real estate entrepreneurs. They offer flexibility and some asset protection. Remember, however, that LLCs do not offer protection from securities fraud.

There are two types of LLC creditors.

Inside creditors.

They can sue your LLC, but not you as an owner of the LLC. For example, someone falls and gets hurt on the LLC's property? They can only sue the LLC, not you.

Your residence and other personal assets are protected from inside creditors.

Outside creditors.

They can sue you, but cannot take your ownership interest in your LLC or take an asset owned by your LLC. For example, if you are sued after you caused a car accident, the victim cannot be awarded your investment in the LLC nor can they seize an asset owned by the LLC.

The LLC's assets are protected from outside creditors and if your LLC is sued, the best your adversary can hope for is a charging order.

A charging order gives the creditor the right to any distributions of *profits* from the LLC; it does not give away cash if you choose not to do so—and the creditor(s) cannot force you to do otherwise.

Further, since profit distributions are taxable, the outside creditor is an untenable possible: You can let the cash build up in the LLC while he pays taxes on it. As a result, the last thing a creditor normally wants is a charging order.

The purpose of LLC charging orders is to protect the other members of the LLC. A foundation of LLC law is to not force members of a LLC to have to deal with each others' creditors. This comfortable level of protection may soon be gone, however, in that a Florida Supreme Court has found that charging order protection is not applicable in the case of a *single member* LLC. There, the court allowed an outside creditor to take ownership of several LLCs owned by the defendant, thereby gaining ownership of the assets owned by the LLCs.

The court ruled that the creditor could gain ownership of the single member LLC (and the assets of the LLC); rather than be forced to accept a charging order, insofar as there were no other members to protect.

While this is a Florida case, lawyers will immediately start to use the same logic to go after LLC interests and assets in California and other states.

Even if you and your spouse are the only members of the LLC, creditors' attorneys will be arguing the same thing, especially in community property states such as California and Arizona where married couples are treated as a single entity. The simplest protection is to add another member to your LLC or a third member if the only members are you and your spouse so that there is an unrelated party whose investment the court would need to protect.

However, never forget that no amount of asset protection planning will do a fig leaf of good against causes of action based on fraud.

Chapter Eight: Remedies for Investors

California real estate investors who want their money have more state and federal securities law on their side than they may realize. *Arbitrary arbitration does not have to be the outcome if you invested in an exempt offering that has gone south.*

If you think you may have been mistreated as an investor in an exempt offering, first find someone who knows how to use the California state securities law ("the Act"), and then determine whether the Act applies to your transaction by reviewing Cal. Corp. Code Sec. 25008.

Note that a sale can be deemed to occur in California even when the purchaser is in another state or even when she or he communicates acceptance in the other state; see *Diamond Multimedia System., Inc. v. Superior Court,* 19 Cal 4 1036, 1050 (Cal S. Ct. 1999).

First Swing under the Act

Often you will find that an otherwise competent transactional lawyer failed to properly qualify an offering for an exemption. You are in luck.

The Act allows rescission of the entire transaction and all money back *even if your case is problematic* otherwise. Ask for a certificate of non-registration from the

California Department of Corporations. Under Cal. Corp. Code sections 25110 and 25102, the folks who sold you your partnership interest or other security must then prove that a valid exemption applied, as an affirmative defense.

Second Swing under the Act

Cal. Corp. Code section 25401 prohibits the offer, sale or purchase of a security through communications that include an untrue statement or omit a material fact.

Remedies under Cal. Corp. Code section 25501 include rescission or a suit for damages.

Importantly, note what is **not** required:

proof of reliance
proof of causation
proof of defendant's negligence

Rather, the affirmative defenses allowed under section 25501 are: a) proof that the defendant exercised reasonable care and did not know of the untruth or omission; b) proof that even if the defendant had exercised reasonable care, he would not have known of the untruth or omission; or c) proof that the plaintiff knew the facts concerning the untruth or omission. See *Bowden v. Robinson*, 67 Cal. App. 3d 705, 715 (Cal. Ct. App. 1977)

Damages Include Interest

In *Boam v. Trident Financial Corporation*, (1992) 6 Cal.App.4 738, the Court held that recovery under the Act **must** be calculated as follows: "Consideration" + "10% Annual Interest" less "Income received" = "Recovery"

Damages Can Include More than Interest

Legal fees will be included if financial elder abuse is shown or as a component of exemplary or punitive damages.

If compensation to the adviser was based on appreciation of the assets, the client must have been a "qualified client" under Rule 205-3 (net worth in excess of $1,500,000).

Offering documents often confuse qualified investor qualifications with accredited investor qualifications— another legal give-me for the investor/plaintiff looking for a securities violation to get her or his money back.

More to consider is the fact that blue sky violations can lead to the law knocking. Most people are under the impression that securities enforcement actions are civil in nature. Although this is most often the case, a criminal prosecution can result if the facts are sufficiently egregious.

A person violates the law if he or she offers for sale or sells any security without registering the security, unless the security or transaction is exempted or the security is covered by federal statute. The Act exempts from registration certain securities, including securities issued or guaranteed by the United States and any state or political subdivision of a state, and other specifically listed types of securities.

Violations typically are punishable by merely fines, albeit stiff fines. However, other remedies may obtain, such as actions to obtain a temporary restraining order, temporary or permanent injunction, a declaratory judgment, the appointment of a receiver or conservator for the defendant of the defendant's assets, rescission, restitution, or any other relief the court deems appropriate.

Chapter Nine: What is a Security?

California Corporations Code section 25401 reads:

"It is unlawful for any person to offer or sell a security in this state or buy or offer to buy a security in this state by means of any written or oral communication which includes an untrue statement of a material fact or omits to state a material fact necessary in order to make the statements made, in the light of the circumstances under which they were made, not misleading."

A security will be found when a person has invested value in a common enterprise with an expectation of profit to be derived from the substantial efforts of others.

This is sometimes referred to as the *Howey* test because of the United States Supreme Court's decision in *SEC v. W.J. Howey* (1946) 328 U.S. 293. The *Howey* analysis has been used by many California courts to determine the existence of a security.) *People v. Syde* (1951) 37 Cal.2d 765; *Tomei v. Fairline Feeding Corp.*)1977) 67 Cal.App.3d394; and *Moreland v. Department of Corporations* (1987) 196 Cal.App.3d 506.)

The second test is known as the "risk capital" approach, first used in California in *Silver Hills Country Club v. Sobieski* (1961) 55 Cal.2d 8111. That decision permitted

the finding of a security when capital was sought from third parties who would be risked in a start-up of a business venture for profit. There was no requirement that an investor have an expectation of a monetary profit from the investment. The California Supreme Court emphasized the passive position as an essential element of the risk capital test.

The Howey and the risk capital tests are not mutually exclusive. Sometimes their elements are combined to determine whether an investment involves a security subject to registration in California. (*Moreland v. Department of Corporations* (1987) 194 Cal.App.3d 506; see also *People v. Witzerman* (1972) 29 Cal.App.3d 169 and *People v. Schock* (1984(152 Cal.App.3d 379.) *People v. Corey* (1995) 35 Cal.App.4th 717 stands for the proposition, *inter alia*, that in a criminal prosecution for selling an unqualified, non-exempt security in violation of Corporation Code section 25110, the element of *scienter* need not be established.

XECUTIVE SUMMARY (write last)

Essential Contents

Provide a brief description of the company's history, if any.

State the company's objectives.

Provide a brief description of the company's products and services.

Identify the market in which the company will compete, including a persuasive statement as to why the business will succeed, discussing the company's competitive advantage.

Provide a brief description of the key management team.

Describe the projected growth for the company and its market.

Provide a description of funding requirements.

Chapter Eleven: Real Estate Blind Pools

What real estate program and type of promotion can be done in California depends on which exemption you want to use, and that decision depends on how much money is being raised, the number of investors being sought, and whether the offering will be in more than one state.

I.   The **California 25102(n)** exemption permits some advertising; $5 million maximum can be raised; it is limited to CA investors who are qualified investors but there is no limit on number of investors.

II. Qualified = $500,000 net worth, or at least $100,000 in gross income and $250,000 net worth (excluding residence), or a business worth more $5,000,000.

ADVANTAGE: TOMBSTONE ADVERTISEMENTS CAN BE USED ON THE INTERNET AND IN PRINT.

Disadvantages: a) Company must be a corporation, not a LLC; b) **not available for blind pools;** and c) amount of investment of each individual cannot exceed 10% of his net worth.

The **California 25102(f)** exemption does not permit advertising but does permit prequalification of investors via Internet sites, blogs and seminars; unlimited amount of money can be raised and there are no financial requirements for up to 35 investors but they must be sophisticated or have substantial pre-existing relationship with company owner(s). As usual, there is no limit to the number of accredited investors.

DISADVANTAGE: REQUIRES (LIMITED) STATE REVIEW OF THE MERITS OF THE OFFERING

The **Federal Regulation D 506 exemption** remains the **gold standard** even for small deals done intrastate, since: a) unlimited amounts of money can be raised; b) there are no financial requirements for up to 35 investors if they are sophisticated or have a substantial pre-existing relationship with company owner(s); and c) there is no limit to the number of accredited investors.

"Sophisticated" = reasonably assumed to have the capacity to protect their own interests in connection with the transaction.

"Substantial pre-existing relationship" = investor knows the company owner(s) well enough to be aware of any problems with the deal.

ADVANTAGE: NO STATE CAN REQUIRE A REVIEW OF THE MERITS OF A REG D OFFERING (AND STOP THE OFFERING)

What else can be done with a Reg D offering?

Page 29

- Pre-qualification via Internet sites, blogs and seminars are permitted.

- Internet links to investor questionnaire and investor statements are generally permitted, but must be completed and returned before offering materials can be made available via password or other means.

- Seminars with only general information are permitted, with questionnaire following. (The SEC has said a comprehensive questionnaire is required, not just box-checking).

California real estate licensee?

California Department of Corporations Release 32-C provides guidance on how a licensed real estate broker can conform to Section 25201(a) of the Corporate Securities Law governing those who effect transactions in real estate securities in California.

Licensed real estate brokers are exempt from being licensed as securities broker-dealers if they sell interests in partnerships, joint ventures, or other entities (other than corporations) engaged in real estate development in California.

These "real estate entities" include entities that a)own land with no income producing capacity and with the objective of holding the land for development; b) own and operate an apartment building or similar multiple-residential housing facility; c) own and operate a building of offices or commercial space; d) own a shopping center or industrial park offering units, sites, or spaces within the premises to lessees while not entailing or contemplating the conduct by the entity of any business within or in connection with the premises; and, e) own motels, trailer home parks under certain circumstances; and agricultural land, under certain circumstances.

If the entity engages in the conduct of a commercial, industrial, agricultural or other business or professional enterprise directly related, or incidental, to the ownership of real property, the entity will not be exempt. Some examples of this are the ownership and operation of a hotel, shopping center, or industrial park where the entity is involved in a business therein; other examples include owning and operating farmland with income derived from growing crops.

Chapter Eleven: Finders & Finders' Fees

Anyone faced with the challenge of funding a sizable real estate project from non-bank sources will consider finders.

The law governing finders depends on whether you are engaging in a securities or non-securities transaction and, if it is a securities transaction, what type. You cannot know what rules obtain with respect to finders until you know the type of offering you are proposing.

If you are trying to raise money from a few active investors authorized to help make important management decisions, the use of finders is unregulated, as long as the finders do not negotiate the terms of the deal and their compensation is disclosed. If you look for money any other way, you will be selling a security.

For a public or registered offering, or a public/private hybrid offering under the Model Accredited Investor Exemption, there is no pre-existing relationship requirement between the promoter and the investors.

However, for a private placement offering management must have a pre-existing relationship with investors prior to the offering.

Supposedly, you cannot rely on pre-existing relationships of finders in private placements, somehow honored more in the breach than otherwise.

The SEC's general position is that receipt of transaction-based compensation signals broker-dealer activity, requiring licensure, unless the finder's activities are limited to merely introducing the buyer and seller.

Therefore, in deciding whether and how to use finders for your deal, the questions you need to ask are:

1) Does the transaction involve the sale of a security or not?
2) If a security, which exemption is being relied on at the federal level and which exemptions are being relied on at the state levels?

About the author

Douglas Slain went to Stanford Law School, practiced real estate transactions and securities law at Pillsbury, Madison & Sutro, and pioneered SBA sec. 502-financing for California redevelopment agencies. Later Slain founded a number of legal publications, including *Professional Liability Reporter, Insurance Litigation Reporter, Medical Liability Reporter, Construction Litigation Reporter,* and *Verdicts & Settlements* (now owned and operated by Thomson-Reuters, Inc) as well as *Securities Enforcement Reporter, Blue Sky Chronicle* and other titles.

Slain has served as the secured transactions adviser to the Ministry of Economy for the Republic of Latvia; taught real estate transactions as an adjunct clinical law professor at Stanford Law School; and served for two terms as chairman of the ABA's largest professional responsibility committee. He currently writes and teaches in the areas of criminal law and practice; exempt offerings and real estate; and cannabis commerce.

Slain and attorney Jonathan Matthews manage an online discussion group with over 550 members (Securities Enforcement Reporter LinkedIn Discussion group) and share a socially-conscious criminal defense law practice .

Page34